SQL FOR BEGINNERS

THE FUNDAMENTAL LANGUAGE FOR DATA SCIENCE TO MASTERING DATABASES. AN ESSENTIAL GUIDE YOU CAN'T MISS TO LEARN SQL IN 7 DAYS OR LESS, WITH HANDS-ON PROJECTS.

ERICK THOMPSON

TABLE OF CONTENTS

INTRODUCTION

MySQL has always been a popular open source SQL based RDMS, which is available for free. In 1995, a Swedish company called MySQL AB originally developed, marketed and licensed the MySQL data management system, which was eventually acquired by Sun Microsystems (now called Oracle Co.). MySQL is a LAMP software stack web application component, an acronym for "Apache, Linux, Perl / PHP / Python, MySQL." Several database-controlled web apps, like "Drupal", "Joomla", "PhpBB", and "WordPress" are using "MySQL. "It is one of the best applications for RDBMS to create various online software applications and has been used in the development of multiple renowned websites including Facebook, YouTube, Twitter and Flickr.

MySQL has been used with both C and C++. MySQL can be operated on several systems, including " BSDI, AIX, FreeBSD, HP-Ux, IRIX, eComStation, i5/OS, Linux, mac

OS, Microsoft Windows, Net BSD, Novell NetWare, Open Solaris, OS/2 Warp, QNX, SunOS, Oracle Solaris, Symbian, SCO Open Server, SCO UnixWare, Tru64. And Sanos" Its SQL parser is developed in "yacc" and it utilizes an in house developed lexical analyzer. A MySQL port for OpenVMS has also been developed. Dual-license distribution is utilized for the MySQL server and its client libraries, which are available under version 2 of the GPL or a proprietary license. Additional free assistance is accessible on various IRC blogs and channels. With its MySQL Enterprise goods, Oracle is also providing paid support for their software. The range of services and prices vary. A number of third-party service providers, including Maria DB and Percona, offer assistance and facilities as well.

MySQL has been given highly favorable feedback from the developer community and reviewers have noticed that it does work exceptionally well in most cases. The developer interfaces exist and there's a plethora of excellent supporting documentation, as well as feedback from web locations in the real world. MySQL has also been successfully passed the test of a stable and fast SQL database server using multiple users and threads.

MySQL can be found in two editions: the "MySQL Community Server" (open source) and the "Enterprise

Server," which is proprietary. "MySQL Enterprise Server" differentiates itself on the basis of a series of proprietary extensions that can be installed as server plug-ins, but nonetheless share the numbering scheme of versions and are developed using the same basic code.

Here are some of the key characteristics provided by MySQL v5.6:

The largest subset of extensions and ANSI SQL-99 are supported by this version along with cross platforms.

Stored procedures use procedural languages that are completely aligned with SQL/PSM.

Cursors and triggers, views that can be updated, support for SSL; caching of queries; nested SELECT statements, integrated support for replication and info schema.

Online Data Definition Language with the use of the Inno DB Storage Engine.

Performance Schema that is capable of collecting and aggregating stats pertaining to monitor server executions and query performances.

A set of options pertaining to SQL Mode for controlling runtime behavior, includes restrictive mode for improved adherence to SQL standards.

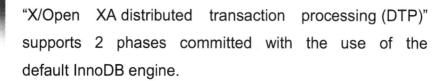

"X/Open XA distributed transaction processing (DTP)" supports 2 phases committed with the use of the default InnoDB engine.

Any transaction with save points while using the default engine can be supported by the "NDB Cluster Storage Engine."

The replication may not be synchronous: owner employee from an owner to multiple employees or multiple owners to one employee.

The replication may be partially synchronous: owner to employee replication where the owner awaits replication.

The replication may be completely synchronous: Multi-owner replication can be supplied in MySQL Cluster.

The replication may be virtually synchronous: groups of MySQL servers that are managed on their own with multi owner support that could be done with the use of the "Gal era Cluster" or the integrated plug-in for group replication.

The index of the full text and search capability, integrated database library, support for Unicode.

The tables can be sectioned with the pruning of sections in the optimizer.

MySQL Cluster allows for clustering of data that has not been shared.

A number of storage engines that allow selection of the most effective engine for every table.

The groups can be committed, and various transactions can be gathered from a number of connections together to raise the number of commitments made every second.

CHAPTER - 1

SQL BASICS

S QL is the most valuable tool used to operate on relational and object-relational database models. Here we are going to focus on what SQL actually is. You need to understand what makes it so different when compared to other programming languages.

Furthermore, you will explore a number of data types and concepts supported by SQL. Before we dive into more complex aspects of the language, you should understand the idea of null values and constraints at a more technical level.

What's SQL?

The first thing you should know is that SQL is not a procedural programming language like C, BASIC, or Java. What does that mean? In a procedural language like Java we use a combination of commands in order to perform an operation (usually several) in order to fulfill a task. This is called a procedure, even if it contains only one command that is repeatedly executed through a loop. In this example, the programmer's job is to plan the sequence in which each command is performed. SQL, however, is a non-procedural language, which means that all you need to do is instruct it what needs to be done. The approach is a direct one. While with procedural languages you have to instruct the systems one line at a time about how your task can be performed, SQL is simply told what to do. The database management system is the component in charge of making the decision regarding the most efficient approach to achieve your goal.

If you have some programming experience already, you are most likely used to working with a procedural language. While SQL isn't one per se, due to a high demand a procedural extension was added to the language. SQL can now take advantage of several procedural features such as functions and "if" statements.

Now let's expand on what speaking directly through SQL means. Let's say you have a table that contains a list of employees and you need to access all the rows that contain data on the senior ones. As a definition for this seniority status, we will take into account an age above 40 or a yearly income above $90,000 a year. To obtain the information according to this rule you need to issue a query like in the following example:

```
SELECT * FROM EMPLOYEES WHERE Age > 40 OR
Income > 90000;
```

Before we discuss the statement itself, you need to understand what a query is. A query is basically posing a question for the database. If there's data inside it that matches the conditions you set with your query, then SQL will retrieve it. Now back to our example. In the statement above we ask for the retrieval of every single row inside the "employees" table. The information in these rows needs to match the conditions we asked for. Each value inside the "age" column needs to be above 40 and each value inside the "income" column needs to be above

90,000. That's it. All you need to do is ask for the data you want and set various conditions to ensure an accurate extraction. Don't forget that with SQL you don't need to specify how to handle your query. The database management system does that for you. All you need is to know the information you're looking for.

Take note that while SQL does include certain procedural features that other programming languages offer; you still don't have access to all of them. This is important because for various projects and applications you will require these missing features that only programming languages like C++ provide you with. That is why you will rarely work in SQL alone. It is common to combine SQL with a procedural language of your choice in order to develop a new program.

There are two methods of extracting data from a database:

1. You can write a query directly as in our earlier example by issuing an SQL statement. Once the query is processed you can read the results. But when do you use this method? Queries are helpful when you need some information immediately. Under such circumstances, you probably never saw that data before and you might not need it again. If this is the case, write a query and learn what you need to know.

2. The second method is more complex than a query. You need to run a program that acts as a data collector. It gathers the information you're looking for and then either print it directly to the screen or in the form of a data report.

These two methods can also be combined for maximum flexibility. You can incorporate SQL queries into such a program in order to execute the same data search whenever you need it. This way you only need to write the query once.

SQL Statements

Working with SQL requires you to know a number of statements. They can generally be divided into three categories. These statements determine the data, manipulate it, or control it. It's worth noting that SQL is a programming language that is very similar to English and therefore easy to understand. Many of the query statements are self-explanatory. This makes SQL very beginner-friendly and easy to pick up.

For now, you should focus on the most important core statements. Keep in mind that SQL has a number of extensions and each one of them brings new statements. The list is quite big. With that in mind, let's look at the most important ones for now:

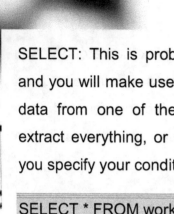

SELECT: This is probably the most important statement and you will make use of it quite often. It is used to obtain data from one of the database tables. You can either extract everything, or only certain parts, like a column, if you specify your conditions. Here's an example:

```
SELECT * FROM workers;
```

Here we don't use any conditions and therefore we will display all the values inside the "workers" table. Here's another example using a condition that involves a value greater than 4:

```
SELECT * FROM workers WHERE experience > 4
```

UPDATE: Another statement you will often be using. It is used to change a value inside a table and update the table with the new information. Let's take a look at an example:

```
UPDATE work wage

SET wage = wage + $200

WHERE worker_id = 123;
```

Here we update the "wage" for a specific record with "123" as its ID. In other words, employee number 123 received a $200 raise and now his final payment is updated inside the database.

DELETE: Use this statement to delete information from a table. Here's how it works:

```
DELETE FROM photos

WHERE photo_id = 99;
```

Here we have a photo with the ID number 99 and we delete it from the photos table.

INSERT: This statement is used to introduce new information to a table. Here's how it works:

```
INSERT INTO photos

values (42, 'The meaning of life', 100)
```

In this example we are adding a new photo to the photos table. The item itself contains three attributes, namely the ID of the photo, its title, and the price.

CREATE: This is one of the most important statements because it is used to create databases, tables, and other components. Here's an example:

```
CREATE DATABASE school
```

ALTER: This statement is similar to UPDATE, however it is used at the database or table, instead of updating values. Let's say we have a table called "class" and we need to

add another column to it, which will contain personal notes on student's performance.

```
ALTER TABLE class ADD professor notes varchar (100)
null;
```

DROP: Similar to DELETE, this statement removes entire database structure elements such as tables or even the database itself. Keep in mind that using the DELETE statement will not delete a table or database. That statement is only used to remove data, not structures. With that being said, let's delete the "class" table with the following statement:

```
DROP TABLE class;
```

JOIN: This statement is a bit more complicated than the previous ones, however it is almost as often needed. As you probably guessed, it is used to combine the data from multiple tables into one. Let's take a look at an example:

```
SELECT * FROM purchases

JOIN paid clients

ON purchases. client_id = paint_clients.client_id

WHERE total_value > 250;
```

Here we have a table "paid clients" containing the data of clients who have already paid for their purchase. It holds two columns, the ID and the name of the client. Then we have a second table called "purchases", which includes three columns related to the client ID, purchase ID, purchase time and the value. In our example we have joined the two tables in order to list all of the purchases that were paid with a value above 250.

There are many more statements and keywords out there, however these are the most important ones that you need to get started. Feel free to explore the rest online, as they are available with a click of the mouse. However, you should pay attention to the way you name your databases, tables, columns, and other structural elements. Some of the names are reserved because they are keywords. Keywords are reserved words that represent the statements we used, as well as others. So, make sure you don't end up in situations where you query the database like this:

SELECT SELECT FROM SELECT WHERE SELECT = SELECT ;

As you can see, it can be quite confusing.

CHAPTER - 2

SQL TOOLS AND STRATEGIES

Installing MySQl Applications

MySQL is one of the tools that Microsoft offers for countless organizations and small businesses. There are several costly certification courses available for a better understanding of the management of these databases.

Here in this book we coherently explain to you the installation procedure after explaining the types of SQL Server editions that are available.

Type of SQL Server Software Versions:

Microsoft offers a wide range of software availabilities for better deployment of the services. It is useless to buy huge resources if there is no enough data. It also doesn't make sense to rely on fewer resources for huge data as there will be continuous downtime which may irritate your service users. For this exact reason, MySQL is available in different types as described below.

a) Express

This is a small comprehensive edition where it consists of simple resources and workbench tools that are needed to start running for an individual or a small enterprise.

b) Standard

Standard version is usually recommended for small business that has moderate data to be handled. It can quickly monitor the operations and processes data faster when compared with the express edition

c) Enterprise

Enterprise version is one of the most used SQL servers all around the world. It has a wide range of capabilities and can be used by moth medium and large companies. It consists of a lot of services such as reporting, analysis, and auditing. Enterprise version costs a lot more than the normal versions due to its complex nature.

d) Developer

This version of the SQL server is especially used by developers to test and manipulate the functionalities in an environment. All the developers use this version to experiment with the logical entity they are dealing with. You can easily convert the license of your developer version to an enterprise version with a click

e) Web

This version of the SQL server is primarily developed to deal with web applications. A lot of medium hosting services use this version to store small amounts of data.

What Are the Components That Are in SQL Software?

SQL Server software consists of various components that need to be installed. Here are some of the most used SQL server managers.

a) Server management system

This is the most important component where every server that is present is registered, created, managed or erased if needed. This is a working interface for database administrators to interact with the databases that are operating.

b) Server configuration manager

This component helps us to give customized information about network protocols and parameters in detail.

c) SQL Server profiler

This is the component that helps you monitor all the activities that are running through the system.

What to Consider Before Installing the Software?

1. Do thorough research about the software you are installing. You can further refer to the documentation or online resources to check minimum system requirements and components information.

2. Learn about components. Get a good understanding of different components such as analysis, reporting that SQL enterprise version offers. Nowadays many industries must analyze and report the findings as a database administrator.

3. Learn about authentication modes that are present and do good research about them.

Installation Procedure:

The following explains how to install and configure the MySQL database in a Windows system. The specific steps are as follows.

1) Double-click MySQL installation file that is deployed to pop up a dialog box and start the installation procedure.

2) once you are done accepting the terms and conditions click the "Install" button to start the installation.

3) After a few seconds, select the "Launch the MySQL Instance Configuration Wizard" checkbox and click the "Finish" button to pop up the dialog box.

4) Use the default settings and note that the default port used by MySQL is 3306, which can be modified to other ports during installation, such as 3307, but in general, do not modify the default port number unless 3306 port is already occupied.

Note: When installing the MySQL database, we must remember the password of the default user root set in the above steps, which is what we must use when accessing the MySQL database.

5) At this point, MySQL was successfully installed. If you want to view MySQL installation configuration information, you can open my.ini file in the MySQL installation directory. In my.ini file, configuration information such as the port number of MySQL server, the installation location of MySQL on this machine, the storage location of MySQL database files, and the encoding of MySQL database can be viewed.

6) When using SQL Server, sometimes according to different needs, server groups are created on the server, the registration server modifies the user's login method and configures the network connection, etc. You need to manually input this information too.

7) In the next step, Enter the name of the server group to be created in the "Group Name" text box in the pop-up "New Server Group Properties" dialog box, and enter a brief description of the server group to be created in the "Group Description" text box. After the information is entered, click the "OK" button to complete the creation of the server group.

8) In the next step, the "New Server Registration" dialog box will pop up. In the New Server Registration dialog box, there are two tabs, General and Connection Properties.

The "General" tab includes setting information such as server type, server name, authentication method at login, user name, password, registered server name, registered server description, etc.

The "Connection Properties" tab includes setting information such as the database in the server to be connected, the network protocol used when connecting to the server, the size of the network data packet sent, the number of seconds to wait for the connection to be established when connecting, the quantity of seconds to wait for the task to execute after connecting, etc.

You should carefully input this information to move onto the next stage.

9) In the "Server Authentication" option area, reselect the authentication method for the logged-in user. After the selection is completed, click the "OK" button, and a "Microsoft SQL Server Management Studio" prompt box will pop up, prompting that the changes made after restarting SQL Server will not take effect.

10) Now click the Finish button in the interface and you are all set to use your SQL server for maintaining network and web application data.

Starting and Stopping Oracle Database Instances

The process of starting an Oracle database instance is divided into three steps: starting the instance, loading the database, and opening the database. Users can start the database in different modes according to actual needs.

An Oracle database instance must read an initialization parameter file at startup to obtain parameter configuration information about the instance startup. If the pfile parameter is not specified in the startup statement, Oracle first reads the server initialization parameter file spfile at the default location. If no default server initialization parameter file is found, the text initialization parameter file at the default location will be read.

The following will explain several STARTUP modes listed in startup syntax respectively.

1. NOMOUNT model

This feature only displays states (i.e. multiple processes creating Oracle instances), does not load databases, and does not open data files.

The code and running results are as follows:

SQL> connect system/sample instance as connect;

2. MOUNT mode

This mode starts the instance, loads the database, and keeps the database closed.

When starting the database instance to MOUNT mode, the code and running results are as follows.

SQL> shutdown {Enter the condition}

3. OPEN mode

This mode starts the instance, loads and opens the database, which is the normal startup mode. Users who want to perform various operations on the database must start the database instance using OPEN mode.

Start the database instance to OPEN mode, and the code and running results are as follows.

SQL> startup

Like starting a database instance, shutting down the database instance is also divided into three steps, namely shutting down the database, uninstalling the database, and shutting down the Oracle instance.

The SQL statement for the shutdown is here:

SHUTDOWN [Enter the parameter here]

1. NORMAL approach

This method is called a normal shutdown. If there is no limit on the time to shut down the database, it is usually used to shut down the database.

The code and running results are as follows:

SQL> shutdown normal;

Database shutdowns immediately with the syntax.

2. TRANSACTIONAL approach

This method is called transaction closing. Its primary task is to ensure that all current active transactions can be committed and shut down the database in the shortest possible time.

3. ABORT mode

This method is called the termination closing method, which is mandatory and destructive. Using this method will force any database operation to be interrupted, which may lose some data information and affect the integrity of the database. Apart from using the database because it cannot be shut down using the other three methods, try your best to always avoid this method.

Launching MySQL workbench

MySQL Workbench is a visual database design software released by MySQL AB; whose predecessor was DB

Designer of Fab Force. MySQL Workbench is a unified visualization tool designed for developers, DBA and database architects. It provides advanced data modeling, flexible SQL editor and comprehensive management tools. You can access it on Linux, Windows, and Mac.

To use it in windows, click on the SQL server studio and select the option workbench to open the interface. If you are using Linux and Mac, you need to enter the command 'workbench' after entering into the SQL instance.

Writing The First MySQL Code

Firstly, when you are trying to write your first MySQL code it is important to get a good text editor for writing down the queries. SQL Software's provide query writing tools for its users usually. It is important to learn about syntax in detail. The first written code is always clumsy and can easily make you lose patience. Also, have it in mind that there is a lot to learn before actually making things better with your code.

CHAPTER - 3

THE DATA DEFINITION LANGUAGE

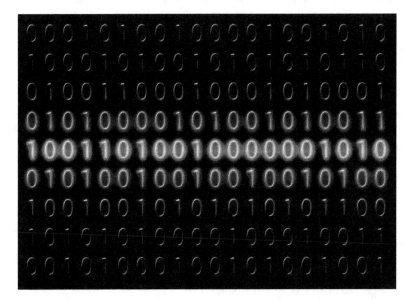

D ata definition language statements are used to create database objects in the database system. They can be used to create table entities such as columns, views according to the specifications given. Data definition language statements are also responsible for the removal or deletion of columns, tables, and views. Data definition statements are user-specific and depend upon the parameters provided by the user.

SQL Essential Objects

SQL objects are an easy way to understand the essence of the language we are dealing with. Just like any programming language SQL too depends on different objects to make a sense for the programmers. Here are some of those for your better understanding of the subject.

a) Constants

Constants in SQL are also called as literal values and describes a constant value of any data. Constants are usually alphanumerical or a hexadecimal value.

b) Identifiers

Identifiers are a special feature developed in SQL for easily identifying entities, indices, and tables in the databases. Some of the well-known identifiers are @, #.

c) Comments

Comments in SQL just like all other programming languages are used to note down valuable information for programmers. Most database administrators use two hyphens side by side to write down comments.

d) Reserved keywords

These are the prescribed keywords defined by SQL software fundamentally and are not allowed to use by any user. Reserved keywords should be referred by SQL programmers from the documentation.

e) Data types

All the values that database tables and columns possess are usually curated into different types known as Data types. SQL offers various data types such as Numeric, Character, and Temporal, Binary and Bit data types.

f) File storage options

All SQL server data is stored using storage options such as the File stream. It uses advanced tactics such as VARBINARY to store the information that is being dealt with. A lot of versions also use sparse columns to store data.

g) Functions

Functions are special characteristic operations that are destined to give results. SQL provides various aggregate and scalar functions for its users.

DDL for The Database and Table Creation

Usually, database objects that are present are divided into two types namely physical and logical. All physical objects such as data that are sent to a disk should be carefully observed. Logical objects are responsible for the creation of entities such as tables, columns, and views.

The primary DDL object that needed to be created is starting a database. Without creating a database there is no chance to create other entities.

Create A Database

Here is the DDL statement for creating a Database:

CREATE DATABASE {enter parameters here}

The parameters that are used for database creation are as follows:

1. Name of the database - This parameter is used to create a valid name for the database. You can't use the same database name that is already present in the instance. Reserved keywords are also not allowed as the name of the database. All database names are stored in system files and can be easily changed if there is root access.

2. Attach - With this parameter, you can specify whether this database needs to be attached to the files of other databases or not.

3. File specifications - This parameter defines a lot of information such as name, size and internal information associated with the database.

4. Logging - You can use this parameter to define the files that can be used for the log management of the system files.

Using these parameters, you can easily create a database according to your requirements.

Create A Database Snapshot

Snapshot refers to the complete visual access of an entity. Database snapshot refers to a physical copy of all the information of a database. If a database consists of huge data, it may take more time to create a database snapshot.

Here is the SQL statement for creating a database snapshot:

The parameters involving this DDL statement are.

1. Database snapshot name - Using this parameter can result in creating a name for the snapshot that you are going to create.

2. AS SNAPSHOT - Using this parameter you can enter the database name that you are willing to create a snapshot for. Remember that the database should be in the same instance for things to work fine.

3. Location - Using this parameter you can give a location to store the snapshot. In default, the snapshot is stored in the temp directory of the system.

Attaching and Detaching Databases

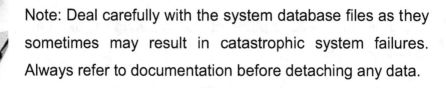

There are different databases in a SQL server and are often required to use information from other databases. SQL provides options to attach data by using FOR ATTACH statement. Remember that if you are willing to attach data then everything present in that database will be imported. This works exactly in the process of merging.

SQL also provides detaching the data for its users. However, you need to look at the database configuration file ' detach_db' for making this work.

Note: Deal carefully with the system database files as they sometimes may result in catastrophic system failures. Always refer to documentation before detaching any data.

Create A Table

Tables are logical entities present in databases. Usually, tables consist of rows and columns and deals with different data types.

Here is the SQL statement for creating a table:

CREATE TABLE {Name of the table} {Enter parameters here}

The parameters involved in this DDL statement are as follows:

1. Name of the table - By using this parameter you can give a name to the table. Advanced SQL server operations also provide options to change column names and data types.

2. Schemas and Constraints - Schemas and constraints are complex topics. But for now, imagine them as an easy way to group objects and provide certain values.

3. NULL - This is a special parameter that helps us to define whether null values are allowed or not in the columns. These type of user specifications are an example of constraint.

4. Tempdb - This is a parameter where all the data, tables and columns created are automatically destroyed at the end of the session.

Unique Constraint DDL in Tables

Constraints are a set of rules defined for maintaining the integrity of the database. These are therefore known as integrity constraints. By using constraints there is a lot of influence on databases and can result in good reliable data. With constraints, it is also easy to maintain a database.

Constraints are usually handled by DBMS but according to SQL standards, database programmers and administrators need to learn about constraints and define them for faster results.

Types of constraints:

There are primarily two types of constraints namely declarative and procedural constraints. We will mainly discuss declarative constraints such as Primary and Foreign keys using DDL statements.

- DEFAULT

This is a special constraint that is used to select columns or a group of columns that have the utmost same or identical values. Unique in the statement defines that the selected columns have updatable and unique values that can be easily recognized.

Note:

Remember that before defining any constraint you need to start with defining its column name.

Here is the SQL statement:

CONSTRAINT {Name of the column} UNIQUE [Enter parameters] {Enter values}

The parameters possessed by the following DDL SQL statement are:

1. Constraint - This will define the constraint we are going to use in this statement. The constraint will usually follow the column name that we are going to apply this on.

2. Type of Index - This parameter on the whole will explain whether this index is clustered or not. Clustering usually refers to canonically arranging index values.

3. Null - You can also use a parameter to define whether your constraint column can accept null values or not. By using this parameter, you are giving additional query information for any further Join operators.

- PRIMARY KEY

The primary key is a unique value that can be identified or used to query with other tables. Primary keys can be a foreign key for other databases. The primary key is usually essential for any database that is ready for query operations.

The primary key as remaining constraints can be used in both Creating and Altering database objects. This is the reason why they are explicitly used to create DDL and DML statements for changing the structure of the data.

Here is the SQL statement for Primary key:

CONSTRAINT {Name of the column} PRIMARY KEY {Enter the parameter values}

The parameters possessed by the following DDL SQL statement are:

1. Constraint - As said before the primary key is a constraint and it is important to define a primary key as a constraint to give expected results. You can also use the primary key without defining constraint but it may often result in corrupted data operations.

2. Column name - In the SQL operational statement you also need to define the column name of the table where the operational procedure is going to take place.

3. Null and Clustering - We will also define whether the DDL statement is willing to take Null values or not.

Some statements will also give slight information about the clustering format.

Note:

Remember that dropping Primary key columns will not delete the created key values but will not result in successful retrieving.

- CHECK

This is one of the most important constraints available because it acts like a schematic operation and will restrict values to be entered. The check clause will explicitly check the constraints that are available and produce results.

Here is the SQL statement:

CONSTRAINT {Name of the column} CHECK {Logical expression}

The parameters possessed by the following DDL SQL statement are:

1. Check - This statement will evaluate the expression given to do a thorough check. Before creating a table or column the database system will look at this DDL statement and start checking the resources.

2. Replication - This is a statement that defines whether the database procedure should be continued or halted

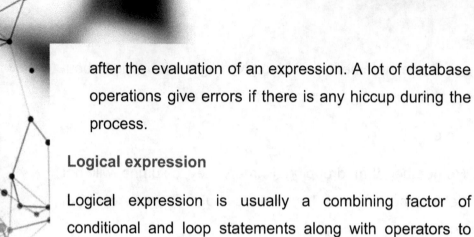

after the evaluation of an expression. A lot of database operations give errors if there is any hiccup during the process.

Logical expression

Logical expression is usually a combining factor of conditional and loop statements along with operators to undergo logical equality or operation. A lot of SQL programmers use this to counter-attack brute-force attacks coming from hackers. When the entities don't satisfy the logical expression then it will result in a halt.

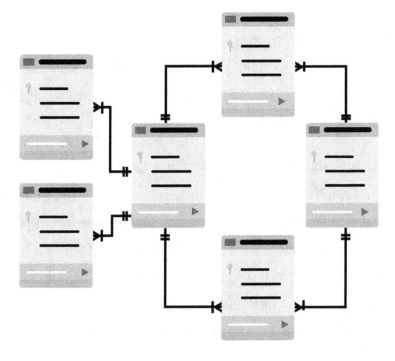

CHAPTER - 4

Creating your SQL Tables

We have spent some time here looking at how to create a table in SQL. These tables are going to be there to hold onto the various types of data that we want to work with along the way. These tables are going to be able to make

SQL work as efficiently as possible. What this means is that you are going to be in charge of creating the data that will go into these tables and SQL can make this easier than ever before.

There are a lot of times when we need to work with creating some of our own tables. We are not going to get very far with some of the databases that we want to create if we do not first work to create a few SQL tables These tables are going to help us to keep the information organized in the manner that we need and will make it easier for some of the searches that we would like to accomplish to happen.

You are able to create any of the tables that you would like, and these can hold onto all sorts of information. Maybe you have a table that is responsible for holding onto your products for sale, and then one that holds onto all of the customer information, and one that holds onto some of the information about the payments and transactions that will happen in your business.

You can then go through and bring up the table that you would like and then search for the information that comes in that table. If you want to look at adding a new product to your system, for example, you would be able to go to the product table and make the adjustments that are needed.

Depending on the kind of business that you are trying to run, and what you hope to get out of the process, you may find that there could be just a handful of tables to get the work done, and other times you will need to have quite a few of these tables to see the work be accomplished. You may need to go through ahead of time and figure out how many of these you are going to need before starting. This will help you to stay on track and will ensure that you are going to be able to get all of the ones set up that you want so nothing is going to get missing in the process.

You will not be able to get things to work as well as you would like if you do not add in these tables along the way. this is the best way to ensure that your information and your data is going to stay as organized as possible and that you are going to be able to get some of the results that you are looking for as well when you do a query and more.

The first step that we have to take here is to work with a new list, such as a shopping list, with all of the items that you want to work with found inside one of the tables in the database. We are going to start this off with a simple list to see how this is going to work, including three items, and the number of each item that you would like to work with as well. This will give us a good start to what we would like to see get done on this kind of process and will ensure that we are going to get the results that we want out of it.

The three items that we are going to work with to help us get the table created here is a blouse, underwear, and pants. We will have to go through and make a new command for the table that will then be able to store this particular type of list. So the sample list that you are going to see inside of the SQL that you are working with will look like the following:

```
/**Shopping list:

Blouse (4)

Pants (1)

Underwear (2)

**/

CREATE TABLE shopping_list (name TEXT):
```

If you place this syntax into the program, you are going to see that the table will have on the right-side column. You only listed that you wanted to have the text inside of the database, and nothing about the amount of the items, so the database at this point is just going to have the list of the things that you want to purchase (the blouse, pants, and underwear). Now it is time to add in the amount of each that you would like to have in the database. We need to add in the integer for this data type with the help of this new code:

```
/**Shopping list:

Blouse (4)

Pants (1)

Underwear (2)

**/

CREATE TABLE shopping_list (name TEXT, quantity INTEGER);
```

Now you will notice here is that when you look at the table, there is going to be a new column that will be listed out in the database that you worked with before. The first column is going to have all of the different items that you would like to purchase, and then he second one is going to have the amount of each of these items that you would like to purchase as well. This is going to be a nice way to create the table that you want to use because it will ensure that you are able to get the unique identifier that you would like to have for these rows, and can help you when it is time to delete or update the rows later on. If you are reliant on just using the rows for your identification purposes, you are going to find that this causes a mess because these values are things that can change for you later on.

After you have had some time to name the rows that you would like to have in the table, it is time to fill all of this in. You will find at this time that the table is not going to have any of the information inside that you would like, and you will need to use the command of INSERT INFO to help get this started. you will be able to set up the first column that you would like to use and then label it as 1, and then the second one is going to be a blouse, and then the third one is going to be how many are inside, which is four. You are able to continue on with this process until you make sure that all of the information that you would like to use is found in the database as well.

To make sure that all of these steps are going to be done in the proper manner, you will need to spend some time creating a good syntax. This will ensure that the table is going to look the way that you would like. The syntax, or an example of code, that you are able to use to help with that shopping list that we made a bit before, and will ensure that everything is in order in the code, will include the following.

/**Shopping list:

```
Blouse (4)

Pants (1)

Underwear (2)

**/
```

```
CREATE TABLE shopping_list (id INTEGER PRIMARY
KEY, name TEXT, quantity INTEGER);

INSERT INTO shopping_list VALUES (1, "Blouse", 4);

INSERT INTO shopping_list VALUES (2, "Pants", 1);

INSERT INTO shopping_list VALUES (3, "Underwear", 2);
```

Once you have placed this information into your new table, you can take a look back at it any time during this process to see how it is going, make sure that the numbers are still the right way that you want. You can even change the numbers, delete some of the things that you are working on, and even add in some new items if you would like to expand the list.

There is so much that you are able to do when it comes to creating your own tables inside this program. While we just started out with a simple formula that has three items inside and a few items of each, you will find that most businesses are going to need tables that are much larger

than this. You will still need to go through the same process in order to get this to work. Whether you just need five items or five hundred items inside of your table in order to keep all of your stuff inside the database, you will find that these same syntaxes are going to work, you will just need to use more of them.

As we can see with some of this, creating a table to work inside of the SQL program is going to be something that is fairly easy for us to work with. It is going to bring in a few different parts, and you do have the freedom of adding in the number of columns and rows that you would like in order to make sure that this database is going to work in the manner that you would like. You do have some freedom later on to make some of the necessary changes to your database, such as adding something new in, taking things out and more. There is a lot of freedom that is going to happen when you work with your own table in SQL, and it is one of the best ways to make sure that your data is safe and secure along the way, and that you will be able to pull it out and use it in the manner that you would like.

CHAPTER - 5

FUNCTIONS

Built-In Functions and Calculations

For SQL, a built-in function can be defined as part of the schedule that accepts zero or any other input and returns a response. There are different roles of integrated functions. These include the performance of calculations, the acquisition of the value of the system and the application in the handling of text data. This section aims to discuss the various built-in SQL functions, function categories, advantages and disadvantages of built-in functions, and types of functions.

SQL function types

SQL functions are grouped into two groups: cumulative and incremental functions. When working in the Group, the grouped functions are executed in different registers and provide a summary. Scalar functions, on the other hand, are performed independently on different recordings.

These are as follows:

1. String functions: they provide a return of a string for any query. They are on select lists, STARTED, INCLUDED and more. Examples of one-line operations include arithmetic_, data mining, time__, conversion_, and XML functions.
2. Added function: When you apply this type of function, you will see the return of a line based on different rows. The aggregation exists in the List Options, SORT AND HAVE CLAUSES. Accompany the group by clause and SELECT statements. Many of them do not take into account zero values. Commonly used include AVG, EANK, MIN, SUM, and others.

3. Analytical function: it is used to calculate a total value found in specific groups of rows. When you perform this function, you provide multiple rows for each group. Analytic functions are the last to run in a query. Examples of analytic functions include analytic-_clause and Order-by-Clause.

4. Function model: found in the SELECT instructions. Examples of model functions include a resume, present and previous.

5. User Defined Function - Used in PL / SQL to provide functions not found in SQL. They are mainly used in parts where expressions appear. For example, you can find them in the Selected Statement Selection list.

6. SQL COUNT function: used to provide the number of rows in a table.

Function Categories

The functions are ordered according to the role they play in the SQL database. The following are some of the categories of functions available:

1. Aggregate functions: perform a calculation on a specific set of values and provide a single value. Aggregated values are used in the term SELECT LIST and HAVING. The aggregate functions are called deterministic. This means that they return the same value when run with the same input value.

2. Analytical function: calculate a total value according to a group of rows. Many series return for different teams. Analytical functions can be used to perform different calculations, such as the current total, percentages, and more.

3. Sort functions: Provide a sort value for each row in sections. These functions are considered non-preliminary.

4. Rowset functions: used to return an object that can be applied.

5. Scalar functions: operate with a single value to return it. There are different types of climatic values. These include the setup function, the conversion function and more.

   a) Configuration functions: provide information on the current configuration.

   b) Conversion functions: change of support data.

   c) Cursor functions: provide information about the cursors.

   d) Date and time data type: relate to date and time functions.

6. Identification of functions: the functions found in SQL servers are deterministic or non-deterministic. Deterministic functions provide the same answers when used. On the other hand, non-deterministic functions offer different results when applied.

SQL Calculations

There are various mathematical functions built into the SQL server. The functions can be classified into 4 main groups, which include scientific and activation functions, rounding, points and random numbers. Although there are many math functions in each class, not all of them are used regularly. The various classes are highlighted and explained below:

1. Scientific and Activation Features: In this category, there are several subcategories. These include P1, SQRT, and SQUARE. The function P1 is used to calculate the circumference and the area in circles. How it works: CHOOSE 2 * 10. SQRT stands for square root. This feature is used more frequently. The function recognizes any number that can be changed to floating data type. Example: SELECT SQET (36) Returns 6. SQUARE means that it multiplies any number by itself. The idea of the Pythagorean theorem is useful here. This means that Asquared + Bsquared = Csquared. This can be done as SELECT SQRT (SQUARE (A) + SQUARE (B)) as C.

2. Rounding Functions: In this category, there are several subcategories including floor and floor. The ceiling function is useful when it comes to an additional number or a decimal number. Your interest is to find

the highest or lowest integer. While the ROOF is the best highest set, the floor represents the lowest set. The ROUND function is applied when you want to round a number to the nearest specific decimal place. This is expressed as ROUND (value, number of decimals).

3. Signs: There are cases that require you to get an absolute number from a number. For example, the absolute value of -7 is 7. The absolute number contains no signs. To help you with this task, you need to use the ABS function.

4. COS (X): This function recognizes an angle expressed as a radius as a parameter. After an operation, it receives a cosine value.

5. SIN (X): This function observes an angle of radius. After calculation, it returns a sinusoidal value.

6. Signal: You can use a signal function when you want a negative, positive, or zero value.

The Importance of SQL Built-In Functions and Mathematical Applications

The importance of embedded SQL functions and mathematical applications

The built-in functions are subroutines that help users achieve different results when managing the SQL database. These applications are used many times when you want to manipulate or edit data. SQL functions provide tools that are used to create, process, and manipulate data. The benefits of SQL in compilation and mathematics are:

1. Data management: Integrated tools and mathematical functions play an important role in data management. Handling big data can be difficult if done manually. This is especially true when the data is huge. Therefore, these functions play an important role in ensuring that your data is handled quickly according to your requirements.

2. Assist in data processing: to take advantage of data. You have to edit it. You may never be able to process big data manually. Therefore, the built-in SQL functions and mathematical applications help you edit your database.

3. Simplify tasks: If you are a programmer, you can make sure that these functions and types make your task easier. You can work fast by applying these functions and formulas to the build. Thanks to these tools, you will complete many projects in a short time.

4. Increase your productivity: Using built-in features improves your productivity as a developer. This is because the functions allow you to quickly work on different projects. If you manipulate the data manually,

it may take a long time before completing a task that ultimately hurts your productivity. However, built-in functions and calculations allow for quick task execution.

5. Save time: Because functions are written once and used many times and save a lot of time. In addition to saving time, the features offer modular programming support.

6. Improve performance: by applying functions. Improve the performance of your database. This is because the functions are prepared and imported before use.

7. It improves understanding of complex logical handling of SQL database is complex tax. Therefore, the functions allow you to decompose data into smooth and easy to use functions. In this way, it is easy to maintain your database.

8. Profitable: because the functions are integrated in the SQL database. you can use them many times without having to invest in new ones. In this regard, therefore, they reduce the cost of operation and maintenance of the SQL database.

Downsides of In-Built Functions

Built-in SQL functions have several limitations, such as:

1. Testing: When using the built-in functions, it is difficult to test your business philosophy. especially when you

want features to support your business philosophy. You may never understand if the features are in line with your vision and business mission.

2. Version control: it is difficult to determine the type of version used in SQL operations. You must understand if there are new versions that can provide the best service.

3. Errors: If there are errors in the built-in functions that you don't know about, they can stop the program. This can be expensive and time consuming.

4. Fear of change: in case of change. You may not understand how it will affect your embedded SQL functions. The world of technology continues to change and this change may affect integrated functions.

Built-in SQL functions and calculations are essential as they allow the developer to quickly complete a task with minimal errors. Calculations in the integrated database make it possible to process and manipulate data.

CHAPTER - 6

WORKING WITH SUBQUERIES

In SQL programming, a subquery is also known as an insert query or an internal query. Queries are defined as queries in other SQL queries. They are generally incorporated into the term WHERE.

The purpose of sub-questions is to return data to be used in important queries as conditions for further limitation of data retrieval. Sub frames can be used in coordination with SELECT, INSERT, UPDATE, and DELETE statements. They can also be used in conjunction with operators such as IN, =, <=,> = and ANTWEEN.

There are rules to be followed by sub-questions. Do they include?

All sub-questions must be in parentheses.

Each query can contain only one column in the SELECT term. This is possible unless there are multiple columns in the important query to compare the selected subquery columns.

Secondary queries that return multiple rows can only be used in conjunction with the numerous value operators. Such operators include the IN operator.

The SELECT list must not include CLOB, ARRAY, NCLOB, or BLOB rating reports.

Queries cannot be included in a set of functions.

Not applicable for the ENTER operator to be used with a subquery. However, it is possible to use the ENTER operator in a subquery.

In the most common cases, subtitles are used in conjunction with the SELECT statement. There are also cases where child queries are used in conjunction with

INSERT statements. INSERT statements use data returned by subqueries. This data is used when importing into other tables. The data selected in the subqueries is modified using different characters, dates and numerical functions.

The questions are also used in coordination with the UPDATE statements. One or more columns in a table are updated using a subquery together with the UPDATE statement. The questions also apply to DELETE statements. In such a case, they are used to remove records from existing tables that are no longer valuable. When used together, they make some changes to existing columns and rows in the table.

There is no established syntax for use in subqueries. However, in most cases, subqueries are used with SELECT statements as follows.

SELECT column_name

FROM table_name

NO column_ name

Expression operator

(CHOOSE COLUMN_NAME OF TABLE NAME THAT ...)

The SQL Server Subquery

When creating a database in SQL programming, initial queries are responsible for creating new databases. One of the best examples is the Facebook application. The application contains some databases for all the following components.

Users: This is a Facebook database that is used as a repository for any information in the user's profile. Save all the details as the person uploads them to their accounts.

Interests: The Facebook database helps to have various interests of the users. These interests apply when monitoring users' hobbies and talents.

Geographical locations: this is a database that contains all the cities in the world where any user lives.

The second query when creating a database is responsible for displaying new tables in specific databases.

Industries that use SQL programming

SQL programming databases are commonly used in technology areas where large amounts of data are used. Some of the most common areas are finance, music apps, and social media platforms.

In the financial industries, SQL is primarily used in payment processors and banking applications. They include Stripe, with which they operate and store data that includes important financial transactions as well as users. All of these processes are compatible with complex databases. Database banking systems generally require maximum security. This is one of the reasons why SQL code has the highest levels of risk compliance.

Some music applications like Pandora and Spotify also require the use of intensive databases. These databases play important roles because they help applications store large libraries of albums and music files. The music stored there comes from different artists. Therefore, these databases are used to find what users are trying to find, to store data about specific users, as well as their preferences and interests.

Social media platforms are other industries that generally use SQL programming. This is because they require multiple data processing. Some social media applications like Snapchat, Facebook and Instagram use SQL to improve the storage of their users' profile information. Such information includes biography, location, and interests. SQL is also applied to these applications to improve effective updating of the application database every time a user shows some new posts or shares some photos. It also allows you to record messages that are generally sent from one user to another. This helps users retrieve published messages and re-read them in the future.

Common SQL database systems

SQL database systems are generally ranked according to the DB-Engines popularity rating. Below are some of the variables that are taken into account during the classification.

The number of system reports on the sites. This is measured by the results of search engine queries.

The general interest within the system. This takes into account the frequency with which Google Trends has been searched.

The frequency of technical discussions for the specific database system.

The number of job offers through which the database system is reported.

The relevance of the database system for social networks.

1. Oracle Database

This is the most popular SQL database system used worldwide today. Many industries use it in their activities.

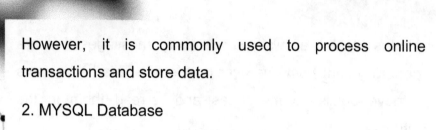

However, it is commonly used to process online transactions and store data.

2. MYSQL Database

It is one of the open source database systems in SQL. It is freely available for companies and individuals. Sit is widely used by small businesses and startups. They usually use it because there is no license fee. It is also used in many open source applications and software programs.

3. Microsoft SQL Server

SQL Server is a modified Microsoft database administration system. It is used in all major versions of Windows operating systems. It is also used in cat software.

CHAPTER - 7

DIFFERENT TYPES OF DATA TO USE IN SQL

N ow that we have had some time to look at the different commands that come with SQL, it is time to take a look at some of the data types that need to come with the process as well when you are creating a new code. These types of data are going to change on occasion, based on the action that you would like to complete on your own inside the database. It can also depend on the products that you want to offer to and even sell to the customers.

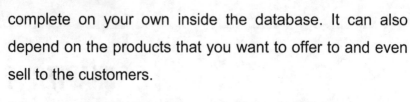

	postgresql	sqlite	sqlserver	sybase
:binary	bytea	blob	image	image
:boolean	boolean	boolean	bit	bit
:date	date	date	date	datetime
:datetime	timestamp	datetime	datetime	datetime
:decimal	decimal	decimal	decimal	decimal
:float	float	float	float(8)	float(8)
:integer	integer	integer	int	int
:string	(note 1)	varchar(255)	varchar(255)	varchar(255)
:text	text	text	text	text
:time	time	datetime	time	time
:timestamp	timestamp	datetime	datetime	timestamp

The different types of data that you are likely to find in this kind of system will be the attributes that can go with the information that is on the inside, and then you can use these characteristics to get things placed on the table. When the characteristics are in the table, you are able to read them, fix them, modify them, and retrieve them any time that you need.

To help us get a better understanding of how this is going to work and why the SQL data types are important here, we need to look at an example. You are working on a program or a database, and you want to make sure that one particular field is going to be able to hold nothing except numeric values. You can use the SQL system to set this up to ensure that if the user tries to put in letters, that the table will make an error or they are not able to type up anything at all and they can just type in numbers. This could be done when you want the person to just write in their phone number, their credit card number, or their zip code.

With this idea, if you have a cell on your database table that needs to just have numbers on it, such as the phone number, then you would need to add in this kind of restriction to the code. By assigning the right data types to the fields that are going to show up in the table, you can solve some problems ahead of time and can make sure that the customer will see fewer errors in the long term.

One thing that we need to remember with this one is that when you work with this system, all of the versions are going to be slightly different, and the way that you do this process, and some of the choices that you are able to make with it are going to change up as well. You need to check out the rules that come with the SQL version that you plan to work with to make sure that it is going to work the way that you would like.

To help us work with the types of data in this system, it is important for you to know the basic types ahead of time. No matter which version of SQL you are working with, there are going to be three types of data that show up in each part, and these include:

1. Character strings

2. Tie and date values

3. Numeric strings

The character strings

The first thing that we are going to take a look at when it comes to data types in SQL is the character strings. We need to take a look at the fixed-length characters first. If you plan to work with some constant characters or even some strings that you want to make sure stay the same all of the time, you have to take the right steps, and use the right restrictions, to make sure that they get saved inside of your system in the right manner. The data type that is going to work the best for this to ensure that you pick out characters in the proper manner includes the following sample:

CHARACTER (n)

Take a look at the example below, and notice that there is an 'n' that we are able to place in the code above. This one is going to be important because it is going to be the assigned length, and sometimes the maximum length, that you are going to allow to show up in a particular field.

Let's say that you choose to use this as a phone number field. You would want to set the n at 10 because that is as many numbers as you want to allow inside of that part of the table. This is just one example of how you could work with when it comes to limiting your characters. This works fine if you want to have the user put in the phone number or zip code, for example. But if you put this into something like the name part, you will end up cutting some people out of the mix because their name is longer than the maximum that you had put into the code.

Depending on what kind of version that you have with SQL, you can find that you will need to work with the CHAR data type rather than the CHARACTER that we did before to set up the fixed-length that you are going to work with. It is often a good idea for you to work with this data type if you want the information that the user adds in to be alphanumeric.

So with this one, you would end up placing the name of their state, but you want to make sure that they are using the abbreviation, such as NE rather than Nebraska, rather than the whole name of the state in this process. You would be able to use the character limit to just two here so that the other person can figure out what they need to do here.

When the data type of character comes up, your user is not going to add in information that is longer than the character limit you set. If the phone number is needed, you will need to set it at ten. If you want to limit the length of the state, you would put it at two characters. It will all be dependent on the kind of forms that you want to use, and the information that is going to become a part of your set of data as you do things.

The variable characters

Now that we have a good idea what the character strings are going to be, it is time to move on to the second thing that you can fix here. This is going to be the variable characters. It is possible that you are able to work with the variable characters rather than the fixed length characters. Rather than only allowing the user to go with so many characters, you can also ask the user to pick out how long this whole thing should be.

This is something that you will want to do in situations like when the user needs to write out their name, including the usernames and the passwords, and more. This allows the user to put in their full name, and then they get the choice of making the username and their password as unique as they will need. To make this notation work in the SQL code, you will need to use the following code to help.

CHARACTER VARYING (n)

Using the code that we have above, you are going to see that the n is going to be the number that you are able to use in order to identify the maximum or the assigned value. You will then need to go through and pick out a form there more than one kind of option that you would like to put in there to help with the characters. Some of the options that you are able to choose here in terms of the variable characters include ANSI, VARCHAR, and VARCHAR2.

For the type of data that we are working with here, there is not going to be any requirement that you have to meet for filling out space. The user is not going to be limited here, which can be nice in many situations. If you did go through and add in a limit of 15 characters, this one would allow the user to write out an answer that is anywhere up to 15 characters. They could also do less than 15 if that is what they want, and it would go through as well.

Any time that you would like to do a few character strings that are going to be more variable, such as a name rather than something like a state abbreviation, you will want to work with the various characters. The reason for working on this is because it allows for us to maximize the space that you are able to use in your database and it can help the user to put in the information in the correct manner,

without any errors or confusion showing up in the database in the process.

Numeric value

In addition to working with the two options for characters that we talked about before in terms of the length of the variables that you do, you will also be able to work with the numeric values and how you are able to use it in the SQL language. It is possible to add in values that are numeric at any point that it makes sense with your code. You won't want to add in numbers during the name point of course, but in other options, you will be able to do it for other parts as needed in the code.

These values are going to be the ones that you are able to store right in the field with the use of a number, without needing to add a character if the user doesn't want to. These values are going to come in with a few different names based on which numeric value you would like to use in the code. However, there are some that are more common to work with, and the options that you can include in your code includes:

1. Decimal

2. Real

3. Bit

4. Float

5. Integer

6. Double precision

7. Bit varying(n)

Literal strings

The next option that we need to take a look at here is going to be the literal strings. These are going to consist of a series of characters, and the length of these will be long or short according to your preference. It could be the name and the phone number that will be specified by either the database or the user based on what you are trying to do at the time. For the most part, these strings will be able to hold onto a ton of data, as long as the data held into it is going to be characteristics that go with it.

CHAPTER - 8

USING JOINS IN SQL

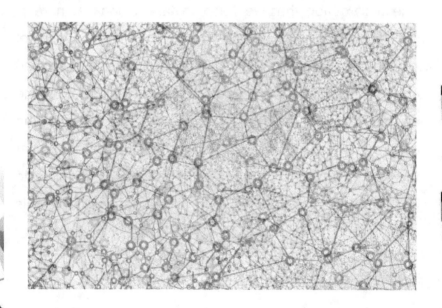

This chapter seeks to inform you about your basic SQL concepts, as well as a quick preview of how you can handle them. When analyzing the data on the SQL platform, sometimes you will need to work on different tables and merge them to achieve the stated goals. The ability to join or merge tables is essential for data scientists, although some scientists don't take it seriously. This chapter will shed some light on the different types of table entries and how you can implement them in SQL.

We'll start by discussing the basics of SQL connections, and then we'll look at the different types of connections that exist today. We will conclude with a quick look at the different types of queries that apply when using more than one table. To understand this topic, you must know SQL beginners and write a simple question in PostgreSQL.

How to set up a database environment in SQL

You should create some tables for your analysis before studying the key inputs. The most recommended table type is one that has at least one column. However, you can apply share queries to similar tables without necessarily creating a new one.

A tool known as pgAdmin appears when you install PostgreSQL to help you perform almost all SQL operations. It is a tool that can be created in a database to create tables in case you do not have a database. The following specs can help you create tables, view them.

name_student (the name or ID) student_stream (student ID)

It should be noted that the two tables share a common column. To create a table, you can apply a create declaration to create these tables. Table entries should have a clear outline if you followed the table creation instructions. In the end, you should have at least two simple tables for this discussion. Having learned this, we will discuss the basic principles of SQL.

SQL basics The joins will let you collate or merge more than one table with the use of primary identifiers. To understand this, let us look at the two tables we created earlier: all of them share and an id column. You might be wondering what the purpose of joining in SQL is? Well, we discuss that next.

Given the constraints associated with normalization, you might miss out on some of the vital information in one table. The process of normalization isn't only recommended but also a must to ensure consistency, bring down redundancy levels as well as preventing various insertions and updating issues. Let's go back to the two tables again, suppose you want to locate the stream in which a student named Sayak has been enrolled. To do so, you will have to merge the tables and then carry on accordingly.

For you two to join two tables, they must be an everyday thing between those two tables. How can this be achieved? Having the two tables share a column with the same name? Or what does that statement exactly mean? Well, we discuss this next!

The tables that are supposed to be joined might not share a column that has the same name, but in a real sense, the two tables should have a common name. For instance, each set of data should have a thing in common. In this case, you cannot merge two or more tables that have a column with a similar name but with a completely different set of data types.

To break this down further, we next discuss the various types of Joins in SQL.

Types of SQL Joins

Here we discuss the different types of joins in SQL joins. We shall discuss each participates to have a clear understanding. It is recommended you first visually study the joins and later execute the set join queries as highlighted in SQL.

The Inner Join

It is one of the most popular types of joins in SQL. For you to understand it better, take another look at the two tables we created earlier. In those tables, the column we are putting under consideration is the one with ID details. In columns where values aren't common in either of the tables, inner join ignores the rest of that column. Below is am executed example of a query where the inner join is performed in between both tables. These are the student name and the student stream. Once you have completed the question is indicated below, you will attain the exact results as presented in the table.

The self-join option lets you carry out the joining process on the same table, saving you the time you spend organizing the final table. There are, however, a few situations where this can be a good option. Imagine the chart you created earlier has the columns consisting of country and continent.

When faced with a task of listing countries located in the same continent, a clearly outlined set below should give you a glimpse of the results expected.

The Outer Join

This type of SQL join can further be subdivided into three different types: the left join, the right join as well as the full outer join. The outer join primary role is returning all the identified rows from a single table, and once they join the target is archived, it includes the columns from another table. Outer joins are different from inner joins in the essence that an inner join cannot involve the unmatched rows in the final set of results.

When using an order entry, for instance, you may be faced with situations where it is inevitable to list every employee regardless of the location, they put customer orders. In such a case, this kind of joins is beneficial. When you opt to use this kind of join, all employees, including those that have been given marching orders, will be included in the final result.

Let us discuss the three types of outer joins we highlighted earlier.

The Left Outer Join: This is a kind of outer join that is responsible for returning each row from the first left side of the table and those row that match from the right side of the table. In case there are no matches on the right side, left join returns a null value for each of those columns.

The Right Outer Join: It is a type of outer join that is tasked with returning each row from the right side of the table and those that merge from the other side (left) of the table. Again, if there aren't any values for those digits in the column, the join returns null values for them.

The full outer join: it is tasked with returning rows from their initial location in the inner join, and in case there is no match found, this join returns null results for those tables.

The Cross Join

It is a kind of join that is essentially a product of Cartesian elements that is expressed in the SQL set up. Picture this; you require a whole set of combinations available between both tables or even in just one table. You will have to use the cross join to achieve that technique. To help you understand this join better, you can go back to the two tables we created at the beginning of the article. Look at both the columns and try to compare the impact each one of them has to the final result. The cross join plays an essential in ensuring accuracy during merging. You ought to note that there are apparent differences between cross joins and outer joins, even though the description makes them almost look similar.

Some scientists have questioned the need to combine data with the SQL joins. Well, this has sparked a heated debate on whether it is essential to do. We shall briefly look at why it is vital to combine your data with SQL joins. To better understand this, let's look at other forms of SQL and how they function. SQLite and various databases like the Microsoft SQL servers related in some way. These databases have made it easier for you to build data tables as well as a faculty to link the data closer together.

Given the requirements needed to achieve a set of indicated goals, the joins are aligned against basic practices to reduce data quality problems. This is done through a process known as normalization, which enables each table to attain a particular meaning and goal. Picture this, you have a table containing various columns with each having crucial information, and you want to change just a section of it; this can be very difficult if you don't have a recommended recovery mechanism in place.

CHAPTER - 9

VIEWS

Views are virtual tables or SQL queries stored in databases that have predefined queries and unique names. These are actually the tables that result from your SQL queries.

As a beginner, you may want to learn how you can use VIEWS. Among its many uses is its flexibility to combine rows and columns from VIEWS.

Here are some important pointers and advantages in using PROJECTIONS:

You can summarize data from different tables or a subset of columns from different tables.

You can control what users in your database can see and restrict what you don't want them to see.

You can organize your database to facilitate the management of your users while protecting your non-public files.

You can modify or edit or update your data. Sometimes there are restrictions, such as access to a single column when using VIEW.

You can create columns from different tables for your reports.

The VIEWS can display only the information that you want displayed. You can protect specific information from other users.

You can provide easy and efficient accessibility or access paths to your data to users.

You can allow users of your databases to derive various tables from your data without dealing with the complexity of your databases.

You can rename columns through views. If you are a website owner, VIEWS can also provide domain support.

The WHERE clause in the SQL VIEWS query may not contain subqueries.

For the INSERT keyword to function, you must include all NOT NULL columns from the original table.

Do not use the WITH ENCRIPTION (unless utterly necessary) clause for your VIEWS because you may not be able to retrieve the SQL.

Avoid creating VIEWS for each base table (original table). This can add more workload in managing your databases. As long as you create your base SQL query properly, there is no need to create VIEWS for each base table.

VIEWS that use the DISTINCT and ORDER BY clauses or keywords may not produce the expected results.

VIEWS can be updated under the condition that the SELECT clause may not contain the summary functions; and/or the set operators, and the set functions.

When UPDATING, there should be a synchronization of your base table with your VIEWS table. Therefore, you

must analyze the VIEW table, so that the data presented are still correct, each time you UPDATE the base table.

Avoid creating VIEWS that are unnecessary because this will clutter your catalogue.

Specify "column_names" clearly.

The FROM clause of the SQL VIEWS query may not contain many tables, unless specified.

The SQL VIEWS query may not contain HAVING or GROUP BY.

The SELECT keyword can join your VIEW table with your base table.

What Is a View, how to Create a View, how to Alter a View, Deleting A View?

How to create VIEWS

You can create VIEWS through the following easy steps:

Step #1 - Check if your system is appropriate to implement VIEW queries.

Step #2 - Make use of the CREATE VIEW SQL statement.

Step #3–Use key words for your SQL syntax just like with any other SQL main queries.

Step #4–Your basic CREATE VIEW statement or syntax will appear like this:

Example:

Create view view_"table_name AS

SELECT"column_name1"

    FROM"table_name"

    WHERE [condition];

Let's have a specific example based on our original table.

Employees Salary

Names	Age	Salary	City
Williams, Michael	22	30000.00	Casper
Colton, Jean	24	37000.00	San Diego
Anderson, Ted	30	45000.00	Laramie
Dixon, Allan	27	43000.00	Chicago
Clarkson, Tim	25	35000.00	New York
Alaina, Ann	32	41000.00	Ottawa

Rogers, David	29	50000.00	San Francisco
Lambert, Janky	38	47000.00	Los Angeles
Kennedy, Tom	27	34000.00	Denver
Schultz, Diana	40	46000.00	New York

Based on the table above, you may want to create a view of the customers' names and the City only. This is how you should write your statement.

Example:

```
CREATE VIEW EmployeesSalary_VIEW AS

SELECT Names, City

    FROM Employees Salary;
```

From the resulting VIEW table, you can now create a query such as the statement below.

```
SELECT * FROM EmployeesSalary_VIEW;
```

This SQL query will display a table that will appear this way:

Employees Salary

Names	City
Williams, Michael	Casper
Colton, Jean	San Diego
Anderson, Ted	Laramie
Dixon, Allan	Chicago
Clarkson, Tim	New York
Alaina, Ann	Ottawa
Rogers, David	San Francisco
Lambert, Janky	Los Angeles
Kennedy, Tom	Denver
Schultz, Diana	New York

Using the keyword WITH CHECK OPTION

These keywords ascertain that there will be no return errors with the INSERT and UPDATE returns, and that all conditions are fulfilled properly.

Example:

```
CREATE VIEW"table_Name"_VIEW AS

SELECT "column_name1", "column_name2"

FROM "table_name"

WHERE [condition]

WITH CHECK OPTION;
```

Applying this SQL statement to the same conditions (display name and city), we can come up now with our WITH CHECK OPTION statement.

Example:

```
CREATE VIEW EmployeesSalary_VIEW AS

SELECT Names, City

FROM Employees Salary

WHERE City IS NOT NULL

WITH CHECK OPTION;
```

The SQL query above will ensure that there will be no NULL returns in your resulting table.

DROPPING VIEWS

You can drop your VIEWS whenever you don't need them anymore. The SQL syntax is the same as the main SQL statements.

Example: DROP VIEW EmployeesSalary_VIEW;

UPDATING VIEWS

You can easily UPDATE VIEWS by following the SQL query for main queries.

Example:

CREATE OR REPLACE VIEW"tablename"_VIEWS(could also be VIEWS_'tablename") AS

SELECT"column_name"

FROM"table_name"

WHERE condition;

DELETING VIEWS

The SQL syntax for DELETING VIEWS is much the same way as DELETING DATA using the main SQL query. The difference only is in the name of the table.

If you use the VIEW table example above, and want to delete the City column, you can come up with this SQL statement.

Example:

```
DELETE FROM EmployeesSalary_VIEW
WHERE City ='New York';
```

The SQL statement above would have this output:

Employees Salary

Names	Age	Salary	City
Williams, Michael	22	30000.00	Casper
Colton, Jean	24	37000.00	San Diego
Anderson, Ted	30	45000.00	Laramie
Dixon, Allan	27	43000.00	Chicago
Alaina, Ann	32	41000.00	Ottawa
Rogers, David	29	50000.00	San Francisco

Lambert, Janky	38	47000.00	Los Angeles
Kennedy, Tom	27	34000.00	Denver

INSERTING ROWS

Creating an SQL in INSERTING ROWS is similar to the UPDATING VIEWS syntax. Make sure you have included the NOT NULL columns.

Example:

```
INSERT INTO"table_name"_VIEWS "column_name1"

WHERE value1;
```

VIEWS can be utterly useful, if you utilize them appropriately.

CHAPTER - 10

SQL TRIGGERS

Triggers in SQL are used to automatically perform an action on database when DDL or DML operation takes place. For instance, consider a scenario where you want to give discount of 10 percent on the prices of all the examination records that will be inserted in future; you can do so using triggers. Another example can be of log maintenance. You want that whenever a new record is inserted an entry is made in the log table as well. You can perform such operations with triggers.

There are two types of triggers in SQL: AFTER and INSTEAD OF triggers. The AFTER trigger is executed after an action has been performed. For instance, if you want to log the operation after an operation has been performed you can use AFTER trigger. On the other hand, if you want to perform a different operation in place of the actual event, you can use INSTEAD OF trigger. now we shall see example of both types of triggers:

Trigger Syntax

Trigger syntax is complex, therefore before seeing actual example, let's first understand the syntax. Take a look at the following script:

```
CREATE    [   OR   ALTER   ]   TRIGGER   [
schema_name.]name_of_trigger

ON {TABLE | VIEW }

{ FOR | AFTER | INSTEAD OF }

{ [ INSERT ] [ , ] [ UPDATE ] [ , ] [ DELETE ] }

AS
```

```
{

BEGIN

The SQL statements to execute ....

END

}
```

Now let's see what is happening in the above script, line by line. To create a trigger, the CREATE TRIGGER statement is used. To ALTER existing trigger, we can use ALTER TRIGGER statement. Next the database scheme and name of the trigger is specified. After that ON TABLE clause specifies the name of the table or view. Next, you have to mention the type of trigger using FOR clause. Here you can write AFTER or INSTEAD OF. Finally, you write AS BEGIN and END statements. Inside the BEGIN and END clause you write the SQL statements that you want executed when trigger fires.

After Trigger

Now let's see a simple example of AFTER trigger. When the record is inserted we will use an AFTER trigger to add an entry into the Patient_Logs table. We do not have Patient_Logs table at the moment in Hospital database. Execute the following query to create this table:

```
USE Hospital;

CREATE TABLE Patient_Logs

(

id INT IDENTITY(1,1) PRIMARY KEY,

patient_id INT NOT NULL,

patient name VARCHAR(50) NOT NULL,

action_performed VARCHAR(50) NOT NULL

)
```

Now we have our Patient_Logs table. Let's create our AFTER trigger that will automatically log an entry in Patient_Logs table whenever a record is inserted Patients table. Take a look at the following script:

```
USE Hospital;

GO -- begin new batch

CREATE TRIGGER [dbo].[PATIENT_TRIGGER]

ON [dbo].[Patients]

AFTER INSERT

AS

BEGIN
```

```
    SET NOCOUNT ON;

    DECLARE @patient_id INT,
@patient_nameVARCHAR(50)

    SELECT @patient_id =
INSERTED.id,  @patient_name = INSERTED.name

    FROM INSERTED

    INSERT INTO Patient_Logs

VALUES(@patient_id, @patient_name, 'Insert Operation')

END
```

Here in the above script we create trigger named
PATIENT_TRIGGER on dbo database scheme. This is
AFTER type trigger and fires whenever a new record is
inserted into Patients table. In the body of the trigger
starting from BEGIN, we declared set a variable
NOCOUNT ON. This returns the number of affected rows.
Next we declared two variables @patient_id and
@patient_name. These variables will hold the id and name
of the newly inserted patient record.

The INSERTED clause here is a temporary table that
holds newly inserted record. The SELECT statement is
used in the script to select the id and name from the
INSERTED table and store them in patient_id and

patient_name variables, respectively. Finally, the INSERT statement is used to insert the values in these variables to Patient_Logs table.

Now, simply insert a new record in the Patients table by executing the following query:

```
USE Hospital

INSERT INTO Patients

VALUES('Suzana', 28, 'Male', 'AB-', 65821479)
```

When the above query executes, the PATIENT_TRIGGER fires, which inserts a record in Patient_Logs table too. Now if you select records from your Patient_logs table, you will see your new log entry.

```
USE Hospital

SELECT * FROM Patient_Logs
```

The output will look like this:

id	patient_id	patient_name	action_performed
1	14	Suzana	Insert Operation

Instead of a Trigger

In this section we will study INSTEAD OF Trigger. For example, consider a scenario where you want to update the price of different exams. You also want to apply the condition that if the price is less than 250, it should not be updated. You also want to keep track of all price updates.

In this case, you can use the INSTEAD OF trigger to run a script that checks If the updated value is less than 250, log into the table that "the value cannot be updated", otherwise enter the value and record the entry that "UPDATED price". The following example creates this trigger INSTEAD OF.

CHAPTER - 11

STORED PROCEDURES IN SQL

Imagine that have to execute large, complex query that performs a specific task. If you need to perform that task again, you will again have to write that large piece of script. If you are executing your queries over a network, you will have to send large amount of data over the network. This approach has several draw backs. First one is that you have to execute complex script again and again, secondly it will consume large bandwidth over the network.

A better approach is to make use of stored procedures. Stored procedure is a set of SQL statements grouped under a single heading. now we shall see how to create, execute, modify and delete stored procedures in MS Sql Server. But before that, let us see what some of the advantages of stored procedures are.

Advantages of Stored Procedures in SQL

- Execution Speed

Whenever a stored procedure is done for the first time it is optimized, parsed, compile and stored in the local database cache. Next time when you execute the stored procedure, the compiled version is executed from cache memory which greatly improves execution speed of the stored procedures.

- Less Network Bandwidth

This means that large complex SQL script is sent to the database over network only once. When you want to execute the stored procedure again you only have to send the command to execute stored procedure rather than the whole script. This reduces bandwidth utilization.

- Reusability

Another advantage of stored procedures is its usability. Stored procedure executes set of statements. Therefore, you can write the statements once and then simple execute stored procedure whenever you want to execute those sets of statements.

- Security

SQL stored procedures also foster security since you can restrict users from executing stored procedures while allowing them to execute other SQL statements.

Creating a Stored Procedure

It is very easy to create stored procedures in SQL. It has following syntax.

CREATE PROCEDURE procedure_name

AS

BEGIN

Sql statements here ....

END

To create a stored procedure, you have to use CREATE PROCEDURE command followed by the name of the stored procedure. Then you have to use AS clause followed by BEGIN and END statements. The body or the SQL statements that the procedure will execute are written inside BEGIN and END.

Now, let us create a simple stored procedure named spListPatients which lists records from the Patients table arranged in ascending order of name.

```
USE Hospital

GO --- Begins New Batch Statement

CREATE PROCEDURE spListPatients

AS

BEGIN

SELECT * FROM Patients

ORDER BY name

END
```

Take a look at the above script, here we started with "Use Hospital" command. This tells the database server that the stored procedure should be stored in the Hospital database. Next, we use GO command to start a new batch statement. It is pertinent to mention here that CREATE PROCEDURE statement should always be the first statement in the batch. But here we have "Use Hospital" as first statement, this is why we used GO clause here.

To create the stored procedure, simply execute the above script. To see if the stored procedure has actually been created, go to following path in your SQL Server management studio:

Object Explorer -> Database -> Hospital (your DB name) -> Programmability -> Stored Procedures

The following screenshot shows this:

Here you can see your newly created stored procedure named "spListPatients".

Executing a Stored Procedure

To execute stored procedure, we use following syntax:

EXECUTE stored_procedure_name

Yes, it is that simple. Execute the following query:

EXECUTE spListPatients

We know that the spListPatients stored procedure retrieves records of all patients arranged in the alphabetical order of name. The output will look like this:

id	name	age	gender	blood group	phone
8	Alex	21	Male	AB-	46971235
10	Ellice	32	Female	O+	34169872
7	Frank	35	Male	A-	85473216
9	Hales	54	Male	B+	74698125
3	James	16	Male	O-	78452369
6	Julie	26	Female	A+	12478963
2	Kimer	45	Female	AB+	45686412
4	Matty	43	Female	B+	15789634
5	Sal	24	Male	O+	48963214
1	Tom	20	Male	O+	123589746

Stored Procedure for Inserting Records

We know how to create stored procedures for select statement. For this purpose, we will create parameterized stored procedures. The following query creates a stored procedure that inserts one record in the Patients table.

```
USE Hospital;
```

```
GO -- Begins New Batch

Create Procedure spInsertPatient

    (@Name    Varchar(50),    @Age    int,    @Gender
Varchar(50),   @Blood_Group   VARCHAR(50),    @Phone
int)

As

Begin

    Insert Into Patients

    Values (@Name, @Age, @Gender, @Blood_Group,
@Phone )

End
```

Take a thorough look at the above script. Here after the name of the stored procedure spInsertPatient, we specified the list of parameters for the stored procedure. The parameters should match the table columns in which you are inserting the data. You can give any name and order to these parameters but the data types of these parameters must match the data types of the corresponding columns. For instance, the data type of the age column in the Patients table is int, therefore the data type of the parameter that matches this column (@Age in this case) must also be int.

Now when you execute the above stored procedure, you also have to pass the values for the parameters. These values will be inserted in the database. It is pertinent to mention that type of the values passed must also match the type of the parameters. Take a look at the following script:

```
EXECUTE spInsertPatient 'Julian', 25, 'Male', 'O+',
45783126
```

The above line executes the spInsertPatient stored procedure and inserts a new patient record in the Patients table where name of the patient is "Julian". To if new record has actually been inserted, execute the spListPatients stored procedure again. In the output you will see your newly inserted record.

Stored Procedure for Updating Records

The stored procedure for updating records is similar in syntax to that of inserting records. In this case of updating records, we create stored procedures with parameters that receive values for SET and WHERE condition. Let us take an example. The following stored procedure updates the age of a patient named Julian.

```
USE Hospital;

GO -- Begins New Batch
```

```
Create              Procedure              spUpdatePatient
(@PatientNameVarchar(50), @PatientAgeint)

As

Begin

   Update Patients

   SET age= @PatientAge

WHERE name = @PatientName

End
```

The following script executes the spUpdatePatient stored procedure.

```
EXECUTE spUpdatePatient 'Julian', 30
```

When you execute the above stored procedure the age of the patient named "Julian" will be updated to 30.

Stored Procedure for Deleting Records

To delete records using stored procedures, you have to write a parameterized stored procedure that accepts the value for filtering records as parameter. The given script creates a stored procedure that deletes record of the patient whose name is passed as argument to the parameter:

```
Create              Procedure              spDeletePatient
(@PatientNameVarchar(50))

As

Begin

    DELETE FROM Patients

WHERE name = @PatientName

End
```

Now while executing this stored procedure, you have to pass the name of the patient whose record is to be deleted. The following script deletes record of the patient named "Julian".

```
EXECUTE spDeletePatient 'Julian'
```

Modifying a Stored Procedure

If you want to change the functionality of the stored procedure, you can modify it. For instance, if you want spListPatients stored procedure to retrieve all the records from Patients table in the reverse alphabetical order, you can modify it using ALTER statement. Take a look at the following script:

```
USE Hospital
```

```
GO --- Begins New Batch Statement

ALTER PROCEDURE spListPatients

AS

BEGIN

SELECT * FROM Patients

ORDER BY name DESC

END
```

Now if you execute the spListPatients stored procedure, you will see all the records from Patients table retrieved in reverse alphabetical order of the name. The output will look like this:

id	name	age	gender	blood group	phone
1	Tom	20	Male	O+	123589746
5	Sal	24	Male	O+	48963214
4	Matty	43	Female	B+	15789634
2	Kimer	45	Female	AB+	45686412
6	Julie	26	Female	A+	12478963

3	James	16	Male	O-	78452369
9	Hales	54	Male	B+	74698125
7	Frank	35	Male	A-	85473216
10	Ellice	32	Female	O+	34169872
8	Alex	21	Male	AB-	46971235

Deleting a Stored Procedure

To delete a stored procedure, DROP PROCEDURE statement is used. The following script deletes spDeletePatient stored procedure.

```
DROP PROCEDURE spDeletePatient
```

CHAPTER - 12

CONTROL FLOW TOOLS

IF statement

In Python, you can use various condition statements. However, you have to ascertain that you follow the Python syntax rules and indentation. One of these rules is to provide an indentation after the 'if' and 'else' statements, when you enter their codes. Simply press the tab once to provide the indentation.

Anyway, the program will assist you in determining errors in your Python syntax. If there's an error, it will display the errors, and what's wrong with them. You can also press for help, if you're lost in the sea of Python lingo.

Therefore, relax and enjoy the experience.

Functions

The 'IF ELSE' statements, which execute codes, are generally used to compare values, or determine their correctness. 'if' is expressed, if the condition is 'true', while 'else' is expressed when the condition is 'false'.

General code is:

```
if expression:

        Statement/s

else:

        Statement/s
```

Example:

Assign a base statement first. Let's say you're teaching chemistry to freshmen college students and you want to encourage them to attend your tutorials. You can compose this Python code:

```
hours = float (input ('How many hours can you allot for
your chemistry tutorials?'))

if hours < 1:

        print ('You need more time to study.')

else:

        print ('Great! Keep it up!')

    print ('Chemistry needs more of your time.')
```

CASE statement

Ruby language is common in organizations for web application development. Ruby on Rails is a structure that allows for rapid development, and business teams focus on other business processes instead of coding functions from scratch. This framework provides a separator known as MVC structure (Model-view-controller). The MVC provides support in separating data, user interface, and business functions.

On the other hand, Python has the most popular MVC frameworks known as Django web framework for web application development. In addition, Python is also famous beyond the domains of web applications. For example, the Pandas library is useful for data preparation. Other libraries such as numpy and stats-model are also

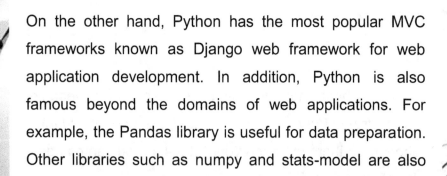

supportive in this case. Matplotlib is a powerful Python library for data visualization. Tensor flow is popular for machine learning tasks and projects. Besides, SciPy is another open-source library for Python, which is used for scientific computing and solving math functions that used to make engineering students sweat.

WHILE statement

The while statement is the main looping statement and is mostly used whenever simple iterations are required. Its structure is as follows:

```
Counter = 10

while counter>0:

    print counter

    counter = counter-1

    print 'Backward counting from 10 to 1'
```

This simple while loop will keep on checking the while condition again and again until the condition becomes false. Until the condition becomes false, every time the cycle goes through the loop. Then after the condition becomes false the interpreter resumes the former activity and continues with the program statements just after the loop. Following diagram illustrates the flow of while controls.

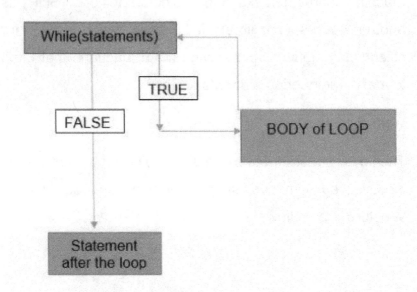

LOOP statement

Loop statement is a symbol used to represent repeated (iterated) word/s or sentence/s in Python programming. Anything that is being repeatedly used can employ a loop (a piece of code). Hence, it facilitates the task that you would want to accomplish.

Types of loops

1. The 'while' loop – this is used to implement a piece of code repeatedly.

   Example:

Let's say you have these values: a – for individual numbers; t – for sum of the numbers:

```
a=1

t=0
```

And you want the user to 'Enter numbers to add to the total.', you write the code for the 'while; loop this way:

```
print ('Enter numbers to add to the total.')

print ('Enter x to quit.')
```

(Now use the 'while' function to allow the action to become repetitive.)

```
while a ! = 0:

        print ('Current Total:  ' , t)

        a = float(input("Number? '))

        a = float (a)

        t+ = a

    print ('Grand Total = ' , t)
```

CHAPTER - 13
CURSORS

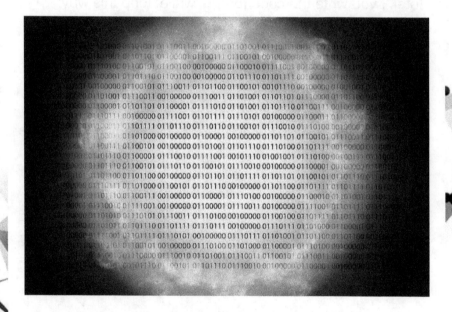

Cursors are database items which are used to iterate over a set of rows and usually perform some extra logical operations or others on each row of fetched statistics. The process of cursor operation entails following tasks:

- Declare the variables to be used

- Define the Cursor and kind of cursor

- Populate Cursor with values the usage of SELECT

- Open Cursor that turned into declared & populated above

- Fetch the values from Cursor in to declared variables

- While loop to fetch next row and loop till no longer rows exist

- Perform any data processing on that row inside at the same time as loop

- Close Cursor to gracefully un-lock tables in any

- Remove Cursor from memory

However, Cursors are typically no longer recommended due to row-by-row fetching and processing of statistics, consumption of memory (due to allocation of temporary desk and filling it with the result set) and occasionally locking tables in unpredictable ways. Thus, alternate tactics like the usage of at the same time as loop wishes to be considered before the use of cursors.

Local/Global Cursor

This cursor specifies the scope and whether this scope allows domestically to a stored procedure or trigger or maybe a batch OR if the scope of the cursor is applicable

globally for the connection. Cursor is valid most effective within the scope defined.

Forward_Only Cursor

FORWARD_ONLY Cursor specifies that rows can most effective be scrolled from first to the end row. Thus, this precludes transferring to earlier or final row and fetch subsequent is simplest choice available. Below is an example of FORWARD_ONLY Cursor:

```
-- ===========================================
-- Author:        Neal Gupta
-- Create date: 12/01/2013
-- Description: Create a Cursor for displaying customer info
--
============================================D
ECLARE
```

```
@CustomerID INT
```

```
,@FirstName VARCHAR(50)

,@LastName VARCHAR(50)

,@City VARCHAR(50)

,@State VARCHAR(10)
```

```sql
,@ZipCode VARCHAR(10)

-- Create a Cursor

DECLARE curTblCustomer CURSOR FORWARD_ONLY

FOR

SELECT

CustomerID, FirstName, LastName, City, [State], ZipCode

FROM [IMS].[dbo].[TblCustomer]

ORDER BY CustomerID ASC;

-- Open the Cursor

OPEN curTblCustomer

-- Get the first Customer

FETCH     NEXT     FROM     curTblCustomer     INTO
@CustomerID,     @FirstName,     @LastName,     @City,
@State, @ZipCode

PRINT 'Customer Details:'

-- Loop thru all the customers

WHILE @@FETCH_STATUS = 0

BEGIN

-- Display customer details
```

```sql
PRINT CAST (@CustomerID AS VARCHAR(50)) + ' ' +

@FirstName + ' ' + @LastName + ' '+ @City + ' '+ @State + ' '+

@ZipCode

-- Get the next customer

FETCH    NEXT    FROM    curTblCustomer    INTO
@CustomerID,

@FirstName, @LastName, @City, @State, @ZipCode

END

-- Close Cursor

CLOSE curTblCustomer

-- Remove Cursor from memory of temp database

DEALLOCATE curTblCustomer
```

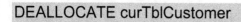

Cursor through default is FORWARD_ONLY, if STATIC, KEYSET or DYNAMIC alternatives are not noted and cursor works as a DYNAMIC one if those three keywords are not certain.

READ_ONLY CURSOR

This cursor is similar to above FORWARD_ONLY cursor, besides that updates on the current fetched row cannot be performed.

FAST_FORWARD CURSOR

This cursor is actually a combination of FAST_FORWARD (#1) and READ_ONLY (#2) along with performance optimizations. Since, it's miles a fast forward cursor, it precludes scrolling to earlier or closing row and being read most effective cursor also, prevents update of modern-day fetched row. However, due to these 2 restrictions, they help SQL server to optimize the overall cursor performance.

```
-- =============================================

-- Description: Create a FAST_FORWARD Cursor

=============================================D
ECLARE

@CustomerID INT

,@FirstName VARCHAR(50)

,@LastName VARCHAR(50)

,@City VARCHAR(50)
```

```sql
,@State VARCHAR(10)

,@ZipCode VARCHAR(10)

-- Create a Cursor

DECLARE curTblCustomer CURSOR FAST_FORWARD

FOR

SELECT

CustomerID

,FirstName

,LastName

,City

,[State]

,ZipCode

FROM

[IMS].[dbo].[TblCustomer]

ORDER BY

CustomerID ASC;

-- Open the Cursor

OPEN curTblCustomer
```

```sql
-- Get the first Customer

FETCH NEXT FROM curTblCustomer INTO
@CustomerID, @FirstName, @LastName, @City,
@State, @ZipCode

PRINT 'Customer Details:'

-- Loop thru all the customers

WHILE @@FETCH_STATUS = 0 BEGIN

-- Display customer details

PRINT CAST(@CustomerID AS VARCHAR(50)) + ' ' +

@FirstName + ' ' + @LastName + ' '+ @City + ' '+ @State
+ ' '+

@ZipCode

-- Get the next customer

FETCH NEXT FROM curTblCustomer INTO
@CustomerID, @FirstName, @LastName, @City,
@State, @ZipCode

END

-- Close Cursor

CLOSE curTblCustomer

-- Remove Cursor from memory of temp database
```

DEALLOCATE curTblCustomer

STATIC CURSOR

If a cursor is precise as STATIC, SQL server takes an image of the information and places into brief desk in tempdb database. So, when the cursor fetches next row, information comes from this brief desk and therefore, if something is modified within the original desk, it is not reflected within the transient desk. This makes the performance of cursor quicker in comparison to dynamic cursor (explained underneath) since next row of statistics is already pre-fetched in temp database.

DYNAMIC CURSOR

As the call suggests, whilst the cursor is scrolling to subsequent row, information for that row is dynamically added from the original desk, and if there has been any change, it is reflected within the records fetched as well.

SCROLL CURSOR

This cursor allows scrolling of rows: FIRST, LAST, PRIOR, NEXT and if a cursor is not specified as SCROLL, it can simplest perform FETCH subsequent row. If the cursor is FAST_FORWARD, SCROLL option can't be used.

OPTIMISTIC/SCROLL_LOCKS CURSOR

Below is a cursor declaration the use of a number of the above alternatives:

```
LOCAL,

FORWARD_ONLY, STATIC and READ_ONLY:

DECLARE curTblCustomerOp1 CURSOR

LOCAL
```

```
FORWARD_ONLY

STATIC

READ_ONLY
```

```
FOR
```

```
-- Rest of SQL remains same as used in
FORWARD_ONLY Cursor
```

Another cursor declaration could use following options:
GLOBAL, SCROLL, DYNAMIC, OPTIMISTIC:

```
DECLARE curTblCustomerOp2 CURSOR

GLOBAL          -- OR USE LOCAL

SCROLL          -- OR USE FORWARD_ONLY

DYNAMIC   -- OR USE
FAST_FORWARD/STATIC/KEYSET
```

```
OPTIMISTIC -- OR USE READ_ONLY/SCROLL_LOCKS
FOR

-- Rest of SQL remains same as used in
FORWARD_ONLY Cursor
```

NESTED CURSOR

As the name suggest, cursors can be nested, that means one cursor could have another inner cursor and so on. In below instance we will use one nested cursor.

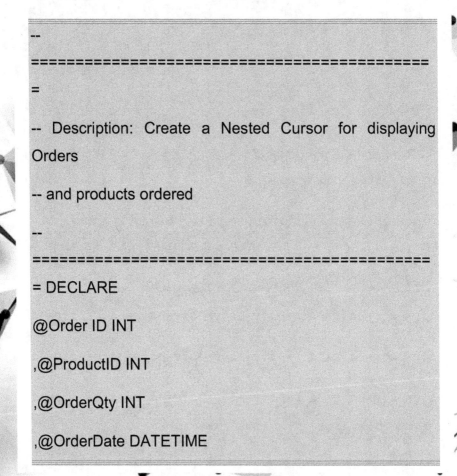

```
--
============================================
=

-- Description: Create a Nested Cursor for displaying
Orders

-- and products ordered

--
============================================
= DECLARE

@Order ID INT

,@ProductID INT

,@OrderQty INT

,@OrderDate DATETIME
```

```sql
,@Name VARCHAR(50)

,@Manufacturer VARCHAR(50)

,@Price DECIMAL(9,2)

PRINT '***** Orders Details *****'

--- First, declare OUTER Cursor

DECLARE curTblOrder CURSOR

LOCAL

FORWARD_ONLY

STATIC

READ_ONLY

TYPE_WARNING

FOR

SELECT

OrderID

,ProductID

,OrderQty

,OrderDate

FROM
```

```
[IMS].[dbo].[TblOrder]

ORDER BY

OrderID

-- Open OUTER Cursor

OPEN curTblOrder

-- Fetch data from cursor and populate into variables

FETCH NEXT FROM curTblOrder INTO @OrderID,
@ProductID, @OrderQty, @OrderDate

WHILE @@FETCH_STATUS = 0

BEGIN

PRINT '*** Order: ' + '' + CAST(@OrderID AS

VARCHAR(10))

-- Now, declare INNER Cursor

DECLARE curTblProduct CURSOR

FOR

SELECT Name, Manufacturer, Price

FROM [IMS].[dbo].[TblProduct] P

WHERE P.ProductID = @ProductID

-- Open INNER Cursor
```

```
OPEN curTblProduct

FETCH NEXT FROM curTblProduct INTO @Name,
@Manufacturer,

@Price

-- Loop for INNER Cursor

WHILE @@FETCH_STATUS = 0 BEGIN

PRINT 'Product: ' + @Name + ' ' + @Manufacturer + ' ' +
CAST(@Price AS

VARCHAR(15))

FETCH NEXT FROM curTblProduct INTO @Name,

@Manufacturer, @Price

END

-- Close INNER Cursor first and deallocate it from temp
database

CLOSE curTblProduct

DEALLOCATE curTblProduct

-- Fetch next Order

FETCH NEXT FROM curTblOrder INTO @OrderID,

@ProductID, @OrderQty,
```

```
@OrderDate

END

-- Finally, close OUTER Cursor and deallocate it from
temp database

CLOSE curTblOrder

DEALLOCATE curTblOrder
```

FOR UPDATE CURSOR

This cursor lets in updating the column values inside the
fetched row for the specified columns simplest, however, if
the columns are not specified, then, all of the columns may
be updated for the row beneath consideration the use of
WHERE CURRENT OF clause.

ALTERNATIVE APPROACH

Note that in above examples, we used cursors to
demonstrate the capability of different types of cursor,
however, we could have used alternative approach, like
using WHILE loop and counter approach to perform similar
task, as became done in #2 above, as under:

```
-- ===============================================

-- Description: Alternative Approach
```

```sql
-- using WHILE loop and Counter Method

-- =========================================

DECLARE @Customers TABLE

RowID INT IDENTITY(1,1) PRIMARY KEY

,CustomerID INT

,FirstName VARCHAR(50)

,LastName VARCHAR(50)

,City VARCHAR(50)

,[State] VARCHAR(25)

,ZipCode VARCHAR(10) DECLARE

@StartCount INT = 1          -- First Row Count

,@EndCount INT                  -- Total Row Counts

,@CustomerID INT

,@FirstName VARCHAR(50)

,@LastName VARCHAR(50)

,@City VARCHAR(50)

,@State VARCHAR(50)

,@ZipCode VARCHAR(10)
```

```sql
-- Bulk Insert all the customers into temp table:
@Customers

INSERT INTO @Customers
(CustomerID,FirstName,LastName,City, [State],ZipCode)

SELECT

CustomerID

,FirstName

,LastName

,City

,[State]

,ZipCode

FROM

[IMS].[dbo].[TblCustomer] WITH (NOLOCK)

-- EndCount is set to total of all rows fetched in above
SELECT

SELECT @EndCount = @@ROWCOUNT

-- Loop thru all the rows

WHILE @StartCount <= @EndCount

BEGIN
```

```sql
SELECT

@CustomerID = CustomerID

,@FirstName = FirstName

,@LastName = LastName

,@City = City

,@State = [State]

,@Zip Code = Zip Code

FROM @Customers

WHERE

RowID = @StartCount

PRINT 'Fetched Row#: ' + CAST(@StartCount AS
VARCHAR(5)) + ' from

TblCustomer table. Details below: '

PRINT 'CustomerID = '+ CAST(@CustomerID

AS VARCHAR(5)) + '

FirstName = ' + @FirstName + ' LastName = ' +
@LastName + ' City

= ' + @City + ' State = ' + @State + ' ZipCode = ' +

@ZipCode
```

```
SELECT @StartCount += 1

END
```

CHAPTER - 14

UNDERSTANDING ADVANCED SQL FEATURES

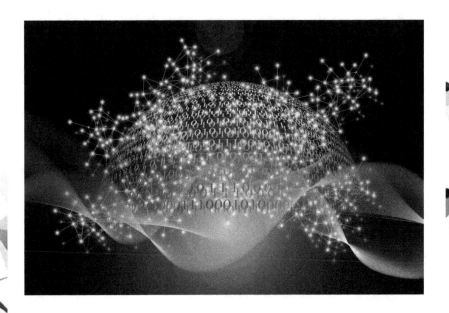

SQL server refers to an RDMS (Relational Database Management System that was invented by Microsoft a few years ago. Seemingly, the primary reason SQL server was developed and designed was to give competition to the Oracle database as well as MySQL. This server has been modified and well advanced

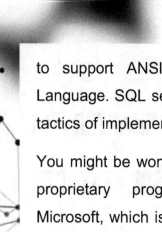

to support ANSI SQL, a type of Structured Query Language. SQL servers, however, are equipped with their tactics of implementing the T-SQL programming language.

You might be wondering what T-SQL means. Well, it is a proprietary programming language developed by Microsoft, which is commonly known as the Transactional SQL. This server has been equipped with the ability to declare variable, exquisite handling as well as stored procedures.

The primary interface tool of SQL servers in the SSMS (Server Management Studio). It has been transformed in a way that can support the 32-bit environment as well as that containing a 64-bit environment. This seeks to discuss more the advanced features SQL servers, and at the end of it, you will have a better knowledge of how it works. Read on to find out!

Understanding Constraints

What are the constraints? Well, they refer to a set of rules that are enforced on data columns of a particular table. They are mainly used to help give a limit to the type of data going to an allocated table. This procedure ensures that high levels of accuracy are maintained, and the means of reading the data in a database is achieved as well. To makes matters better, these constraints can be

packaged either at table level or at a column level. To break it down further, the restrictions applied in the column level can be used only on one set of the column, while those in the table level can be used on the entire table.

Written below are some of the popular constraints used in the SQL programming language. The 'Not Null Constraint' - This type of constraint ensures that every column only has a NULL value in the table.

- The 'Default Constraints' - This is a type of constraint that provides a primary figure for each column where none of them has been classified.
- The 'Unique Constraints'- This type of constraint makes sure that every value in the table or column has different criteria.

Additionally, the foreign key is an essential part of this process; this is because it is used to identify a set of rows or records in any provided database tables.

The Check constraint is also another kind of these elements. Its significant role in ensuring that every value in the column has satisfied the set conditions. The index, on the other hand, can be used to build and create from the operating databases in very efficient ways. When faced with a situation where you have to specify the constraints, it can be done so through a type of table that has been built via 'create table' statement, and you can as well apply the using alter table statements to come up with your constraints even when the table has already been created.

Dropping the Constraints

This subtopic will help you understand the process of dropping a constraint. Note that any kind of constraint you created earlier on can left alone or somewhat dropped from the system via the Alter Table command, which contains the Drop Constant options. For instance, if you wish to drop a primary key constraint that involves the employees' table, you can do so through the command 'Alt Table Employees Drop Const Employ_PK.

The command could result in implementations that might as give a provision to the shortcut measures that contain procedures necessary for dropping constraints. Let's look at the following example: to let go of a kind of primary constraint located in an Oracle table, you can still use the command we have highlighted above to drop it.

Additionally, some implementations might result in you disabling the functioning constraints. When faced with an occurrence of deciding whether to drop a restriction from the database permanently, you can opt for temporal disabling and later on enable it.

Talking of constraints, we must discuss the integrity constraints. They are an essential part of this subject and applied in several fields. First, they are applied to ensuring there is adequate accuracy and reasonable consistency in the manner data is applied in the relational databases. It plays a critical role by providing information that is efficiently handled through the known ideology of referential integrity.

There exist various types of constraints that are involved in Referential Integrity. The obstacles involved are the based key, the foreign key as well as the unique one.

Understanding Indexes

A database index refers to a feature that lets you perform a query to retrieve data from a database more efficiently. A typical index contains a number of relatable specified tables and contains more than one key. Similarly, a table can have a more set of indexes than it was initially built to provide. You should, however, note that keys are mainly based on the columns created by comparing the keys and allocated indexes. By doing so, it is easier to ensure each database contains a similar amount of data value.

Indexes, can quickly speed up the process of retrieving data. It is, therefore, important to first modify and correct the indexes as required by each table. In smaller databases, missing indexes will not be shown, and you can be assured that once the table starts increasing in size, the queries applied will take a longer time to occur.

When working on a set of databases in which the period of operating on them is roughly around eight days to get it done, it will force you to come up with measures that bring down the period to a shorter period. As a way of achieving that, you can choose to run the database through a query plan developer who can benefit both of the new indexes. This had proven to be very efficient because, from an estimated three hundred thousand operations, the procedure will cut it down to only thirty! This can consequently cut down the number of days you had to work on it from eight to just two hours. Therefore, indexes are much more efficient when it comes to boosting the speed of performance.

Understanding Triggers

When downloading the SQL database files on a Windows computer, you will come across two different kits: the first one on which the systems run containing the Sun Java SDK and the other one that doesn't include the Sun Java SDK. Be assured you are downloading the right file first before installing it. You are welcome to confirm from the upcoming part of this section vital instructions and requirements needed to install the SQL server.

To begin with, the procedure of installing a SQL database mainly depends on one thing: whether or not the Windows system in use doesn't contain the Sun Java SDK. When working on a Windows system with the release 1.5.0_06 or installed later, every other system, including the Mac OS and Linux that have no Java SDK.

Below we discuss ways you can install the SQL servers on any computer, be it Windows or Linux. Read on to find out!

When you want to run and install your SQL developer on Windows operating systems, and the Java script involved is more than the normal update 6, you are recommended to implement the following steps.

Start by unzipping the SQL developer file to the folder you have preferred. For an occurrence, it can be C:\Program Files. On other computers, it can also be referred to as the SQL developer installer. Once you have unzipped the kit containing the SQL developer, it will trigger a folder named the sqldevlp to be established the installed SQL file formed earlier. It will also result in various folders and files to be located in the same directory. If you wish to start running this SQL developer, it is recommended you go to the previously installed SQL folder and then click the sqldevlper.exe. File.

Upon clicking, you will be asked to key in the name for your Java file downloaded earlier, then proceed to click the known corresponding file named program files java folds. When the SQL developer database starts operating, you can as well link to a database of your choice by only right-clicking the connections option in the known connections navigator, then following it up by choosing a new connection model. Similarly, if you had a few exported connections in the database, it is recommended you import those connections and put them into use.

CHAPTER - 15

EXERCISES AND PROJECTS

W e are going to perform exercises and projects that will help sharpen our skills in this section.

Exercise 1

Using the DVDRental database, retrieve the first 20 film titles that had a rental_duration of less than 6.

Sample Solution

You can retrieve the film titles using the conditional check with the SQL WHERE statement. The simplest way is:

```
SELECT t.title FROM public.film t WHERE rental_duration
< 6 LIMIT 20;
```

NOTE: To ensure that you use your own method to retrieve the data, I have used a different syntax.

Exercise 2.

Retrieve the Customer IDs of the customers who have spent at least 110.

Sample Solution

You can also get all the IDs of the customers who have used at least 110 dollars.

The sample code would be:

```
SELECT customer_id,SUM(amount)
FROM public.payment
GROUP BY customer_id
HAVING SUM(amount) > 110;
```

Exercise 3

Get the total number of films that has a title that start with the later 'A'

Sample Solution

```
SELECT * FROM film
WHERE title LIKE 'A%';
```

An Interactive SQL Project

In this section, we are going to practice the process of creating a database from scratch and then adding data and primary keys maintaining data integrity.

Step 1

Create a fresh new database and name it as PractiseDb. Do not use the graphical control (pgAdmin) for this part.

```
create database Practise_Db;
```

Step 2:

Using one SQL script, create a new database schema and name it practice_schema. Next, using the schema created, add a table, and add a description as follows "a table to store product information"   .

In the above table, create five different columns as follows: product_id, product_name, department, price, and date.

Set the data type of the above columns as follows (respectively): integer, text, text, money, and date. Set the product_id as the product key. The following columns MUST be set to contain no NULL value (meaning cannot be empty): product_id, date, product_name.

Add a relationship (foreign key) from product_id to product_name and set the delete rule to restrict.

NOTE: Use the SQL commands and not pgAdmin. A sample code is below:

```
create table practise_store
(
    product_id   integer not null
        constraint practise_store_pk
            primary key,
    product_name text    not null,
    department   text    not null,
    price        money,
    date         date    not null
);
comment on table practise_store is 'a table to store
information';
alter table practise_store
    owner to postgres;
create unique index practise_store_product_id_uindex
    on practise_store (product_id);
```

Once you have created a database, a database schema, tables and columns, launch pgAdmin and enter sample data to the columns. Intentionally experiment with the database using the knowledge you have distilled from this guide; for instance, you can try adding a text to the product_id column.

CONCLUSION

Although it can be much to learn, SQL can be a very simple language to use in a database.

By taking advantage of the necessary tools in this book, you can successfully maneuver your way throughout any database.

It is necessary to keep in mind that not all formulas work the same in every database, and there are different versions listed in the book.

There is plenty to learn when it comes to SQL, but with the use of practice and good knowledge, you can be as successful as you decide to be in any database.

Just how the English language has many rules to be followed, the same applies to SQL.

By exercising the time to learn the language thoroughly, many things are achievable with the use of a database.

Refer back to any of the information in this book any time you are stumped on something; you are working on.

Although it can be a complex challenge, patience and practice will help you successfully learn SQL.

By remembering the basic commands and rules to SQL, you will avoid any issues that can come across most individuals that practice the use of it.

It is a lot of information to take in, but instead, take it as it comes.

Go to the practical tools that you may need for whatever you are trying to achieve through the database.

When presented with an obstacle or complex assignment, refer to the tools that will clear up what you need.

Take time to fully analyze what is before you while also trying to focus on one thing at a time.

Keep an open and simple mind when moving forward, and you will keep any issues from becoming more complicated than what they need to be.

As mention, SQL can be a simple thing to learn.

You simply need to take the time to understand what everything fully means in-depth.

If something doesn't turn out as expected, retrace your tracks to find where you might have inappropriately added formula and some of the information.

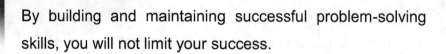

By building and maintaining successful problem-solving skills, you will not limit your success.

It Is All About Asking Good Questions

If you have gone this far, you have seen how we can use Structured Query Language to turn lifeless entries in a database into meaningful information that you or your company can use to make the tough decisions that define every business venture.

Throughout this book, I have tried to demonstrate how to write efficient but intelligent queries using real-world scenarios that showcase the methods that I have found useful and still use today.

I did my best to avoid the philosophical debates, technicalities, and academic jargon that plague everybody of technical knowledge in order to bring you by the purest and most expedient path to your own unique mastery of SQL.

To the beginner: I hope you have enjoyed this journey we have taken together and that I have built a bridge for you to continue on your path to data mastery.

To those with previous experience: I hope this book has highlighted a few insights and given you a sandbox to test your ever-growing SQL toolbox.

Choosing the Right Database Occupation

Although we have focused mainly on the role of the database analyst (using your skills in query composition, composing statements, and answering everyday questions), there is plenty of demand for database designers as well.

If you have ever wondered who decides what fields will be contained in any given table, or how the tables will relate to each other, that is the job of a database designer/modeler.